Lady
GAGA

A MONSTER ROMANCE

Publisher and Creative Director: Nick Wells
Project Editors: Polly Prior and Catherine Taylor
Picture Research: Laura Bulbeck
Art Director and Layout Design: Mike Spender
Digital Design and Production: Chris Herbert

Special thanks to: Stephen Feather, Karen Fitzpatrick and Dawn Laker

FLAME TREE PUBLISHING
Crabtree Hall, Crabtree Lane
Fulham, London SW6 6TY
United Kingdom

www.flametreepublishing.com

First published 2012

12 14 16 15 13
1 3 5 7 9 10 8 6 4 2

Flame Tree Publishing is part of The Foundry Creative Media Co. Ltd

A CIP record for this book is available from the British Library upon request.

ISBN 978-0-85775-276-5

Printed in China

HUGH FIELDER

Lady
GAGA

A MONSTER ROMANCE

FOREWORD BY MALCOLM MACKENZIE,
EDITOR, *WE LOVE POP* MAGAZINE

FLAME TREE
PUBLISHING

Contents

Foreword

For me there is no competition: Lady Gaga is the best pop star in the world.
Not since the 1980s heyday of Michael Jackson, Madonna and Prince has a pop icon inspired global devotion like Stefani Germanotta.

I was a fan from the moment I heard breezy debut single 'Just Dance' at the tail end of 2008. I went to see her very first club appearance at the Astoria in London, right before they tore it down. Despite brandishing her disco stick clumsily in roughly made iPod specs to a half empty auditorium, you could see she was a bit special. But when I first interviewed her I never dreamed she would become the mega-selling, taboo-busting, gender-swapping, generation-defining, record-breaking, smoldering fag-end, beef-fillet and Kermit-the-Frog-wearing artist she is today. Or that she would go on to produce three incredible albums in three short years.

Gaga has succeeded in changing the landscape of popular music. We can categorize music in the twenty-first century as BG and PG: Before-Gaga and Post-Gaga. It is no longer acceptable to turn up, sing a nice song and bob about from side to side on the stage as many artists did in the world BG. Gaga brought back drama and everyone looked drab in comparison. Suddenly her pop peers stepped up their game and became the best versions of themselves that they could.

But behind the image lies a unique voice and writing talent; Gaga is as comfortable singing jazz standards with Tony Bennett and knocking out piano ballads for Queen Elizabeth as she is spitting blood and making out with maligned religious figures. She is in a constant state of metamorphosis – some ideas work better than others – but we are always glad she made the effort. Put your paws up for Mother Monster.

Malcolm Mackenzie
Editor, *We Love Pop* magazine

Making Records

Three years after an unknown Lady Gaga released her first record in June 2008 she had sold more than 17 million albums and over 50 million singles worldwide. Those figures would have been impressive back in the 1980s when pop icons such as Madonna and Michael Jackson reigned supreme, but some 30 years later with the record industry seemingly in commercial meltdown, those numbers are astounding.

When *The Fame* (2008) was released in the US it sold 24,000 copies in the first week and entered the charts at No. 17. It didn't go higher than No. 4 but never fell too far down the charts either. US sales have now passed 4.4 million including 961,000 digital copies, making it second best-selling digital album (behind Eminem's *Recovery* (2010)). Worldwide sales have already passed 12 million.

Breaking Records

When *Born This Way* (2011) was released it shot straight to No. 1 in the US, with first-week sales of more than 1.1 million, the highest weekly total in seven years, and more than the next 42 albums in the chart combined. Within four months *Born This Way* sold five million copies worldwide.

'I'm trying to give people things that they don't need but will eventually become the reality of the future.

Lady Gaga

'I don't want to sound presumptuous but I've made it my goal to revolutionize pop music.'

Lady Gaga

It is not just Lady Gaga's albums that break records; she is the first artist to sell 20 million digital singles in America; 'Bad Romance' sold 9.7 million digital copies in 2010, followed by 'Telephone' with 7.4 million. And 'Poker Face' was the most downloaded single of 2009. Lady Gaga was still breaking digital records in 2011. 'Born This Way' was the fastest-selling single in the history of iTunes. In five days users of the online store downloaded the song over a million times.

And The Winner Is . . .

A grateful music industry has been quick to shower Lady Gaga with awards for her achievements. She already has five American Grammies for Best Electronic Dance Album 2009 (*The Fame*), Best Dance Recording 2010 ('Poker Face'), Best Pop Vocal Album 2011 (*The Fame Monster*), Best Female Pop Vocal Performance and Best Video 2011 ('Bad Romance'). She also won three BRIT Awards in 2010 for Female Solo Artist, International Breakthrough Act and Best International Album, along with five gongs from the World Music Awards as well as 23 MTV awards from around the world.

Fashion industry awards are not far behind. The Council of Fashion Designers of America gave her the Fashion Icon Award in 2011. And the readers of fashionable *NME* magazine managed to vote Lady Gaga Best Dressed and Worst Dressed in 2010, without a trace of irony.

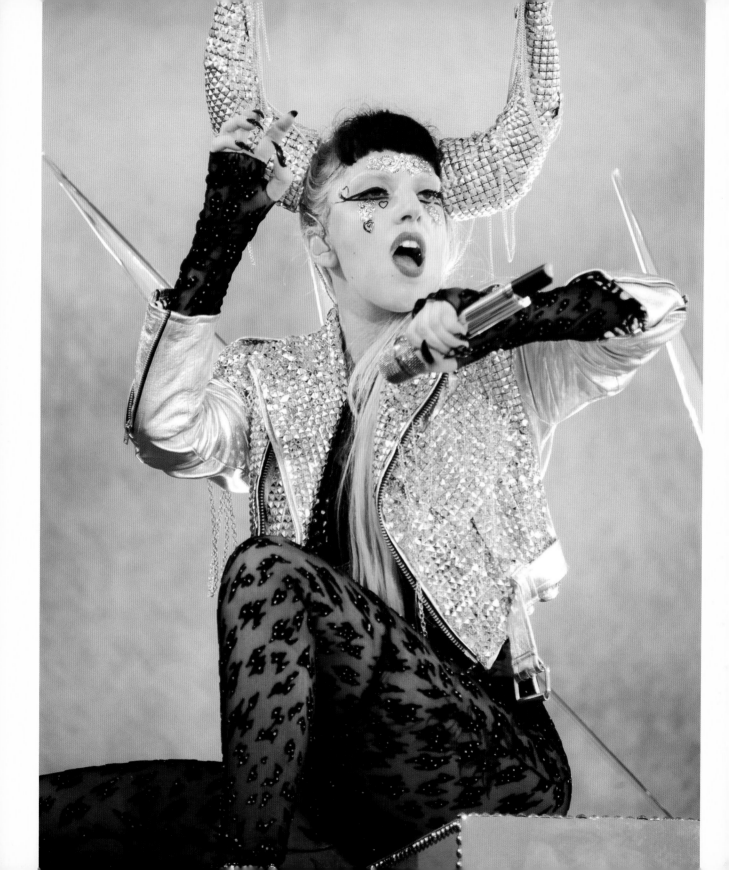

'I'm an outcast from the music industry. I don't have any friends in the business. I feel completely detached from the celebrity world. You never see me falling out of nightclubs.'

Lady Gaga

Beautiful Dirty Rich

It can be hard to separate fact from fiction when it comes to rock star earnings, but the highly regarded *Forbes* magazine estimated Lady Gaga's 2010 earnings at $62 million, putting her 14th on the magazine's list of top-earning entertainers. *Forbes* also placed Lady Gaga top of their list of the world's most powerful celebrities for 'reinvigorating pop music and pop culture'. Her earnings for 2011 are likely to exceed $100 million.

Lady Gaga claims not to be interested in her riches. 'Money is completely boring to me,' she says. 'It means nothing, except it feeds my art.' One part of her art that requires considerable feeding is the Haus Of Gaga: a team of designers who work on her stage sets, costumes, jewellery and what she calls 'the concept of Gaga'.

'The only big things I've purchased are my dad's heart valve and a Rolls Royce for their anniversary.'

Lady Gaga

Why Gaga?

The public rise of Lady Gaga may only have taken three years, but in reality the project has been going on inside her head for much longer. As the lady says, 'I've been doing this since I was 14'. The seven years she spent developing the character were crucial; she developed an invulnerable self-belief that has helped her to withstand the whirlwind that struck almost as soon as Lady Gaga 'went public'.

This has been most evident in her fast-evolving image, which has changed with almost every single release, from the Hollywood party kid on 'Just Dance' to the Martian queen on 'Poker Face' to subway-dancing pop star on 'LoveGame' to full-blown celebrity on 'Paparazzi'. The changes were, of course, deliberate. She says, 'There's never a reason to do something unless it's going to be memorable.'

'She's definitely a big style icon for everyone and it's made everyone go a bit more edgy with their fashion.'
Naomi Campbell

> '*Some people are just born stars. You either have it or you haven't, and I was definitely born one.*'
>
> *Lady Gaga*

24/7 Work Ethic

Along with her unshakeable self-belief, Lady Gaga has a relentless work ethic that focuses exclusively on herself. Her manager, Troy Carter, says, 'One of the problems now is that we have a very lazy business. That girl gets out there.' Lady Gaga has her own way of dealing with those mornings when you just don't feel like it. 'I say, "Bitch, you're Lady Gaga. You get up and walk the walk today".'

She refuses to play safe in a world of plastic pop stars and doesn't try to compete with other successful artists such as Beyoncé or Katy Perry. She is offering something different: her own mix of glam rock with pop melodies. While other pop stars call on tried-and-trusted hit-making producers as soon as they can afford to, Lady Gaga deliberately chooses to work with relatively unknown producers, because they share her hunger.

Meticulous Marketing

The success of *The Fame* was down to the music and Lady Gaga's willingness to tour round the world and play for the fans. However, a meticulous campaign was devised for *Born This Way*: she announced the title at the MTV Video Music Awards, premiered the title track at the Grammy Awards and performed 'The Edge Of Glory' at the final of *American Idol*. If the public missed any of those marketing ploys, there was

'I'm not one of those self-obsessed artists who don't care about their fans. I look out into the O2 Arena and there are 18,000 screaming young people and I have a responsibility to them. You're an idiot if you don't know that.'

Lady Gaga

also a live concert on the HBO channel, the Gagaville online game and New York subway carriages decked out with 'Born This Way' advertising.

Right behind the power of her music comes Lady Gaga's charismatic live performance. Like Madonna and Michael Jackson she knows how to excite and captivate an audience, whether it's her personalized version of John Lennon's 'Imagine' at the Human Rights Campaign's annual dinner or the theatrical excesses of 'The Edge Of Glory' on *American Idol*.

Little Monsters

More important than just the adulation, Lady Gaga knows that a strong, loyal fan base is essential to sustain a pop career. Hit songs are meaningless if there is no lasting attachment to the artist. Dedicated fans can offer limitless free advertising; that is perhaps one reason why Lady Gaga is completely committed to her fans, or 'little monsters' as she calls them.

She knows exactly how to speak to her millions of followers on Twitter, and her fans are the first to be told about new single and album release dates. They even got to see the 'Bad Romance' video before anyone else when she released it on her own website. While the record industry gets paranoid about people downloading music and videos, Lady Gaga leaves everything up there for the internet to do what the internet does best – spread the information at the speed of light.

'I saw her on the America Music Awards and I was like, "You're an animal of another kind and we need you".'

Katy Perry

Under The Influence

No sooner had Lady Gaga released 'Just Dance' than the critics started making comparisons. Back then it was to Christina Aguilera and Paris Hilton – because American critics had never heard of British electro-pop.

Lady Gaga has never denied any of the artists who have influenced her. Here is a list she posted on her myspace site: Yoko Ono, Elvis, David Bowie, Morrissey, Queen, Robert Smith, Robert Plant, Freddie Mercury, Prince, Rod Stewart, Thomas Dolby, Depeche Mode, The Faint, Radiohead, Beck, Franz Ferdinand, The Cure, Nine Inch Nails, Grace Slick and Jefferson Airplane, Led Zeppelin, Pink Floyd, Nirvana, Talking Heads, Scissor Sisters, The Dresden Dolls, Mika, She Wants Revenge, Janis Joplin, Jenny Lewis, Joy Division, New Order, The Killers, Justin Warfield, Chuck Berry, Buckcherry, Billy Idol, The White Stripes, The Strokes, Blondie, Pat Benatar, Rilo Kiley, Elton John, Jerry Lee Lewis, John Lennon, The Beatles.

The Material Girl

As the biggest pop icon of the twentieth century, comparisons with Madonna are inevitable. And the similarities go more than skin deep. Both grew up in Catholic Italian-American families, both started out on the New York underground scene, and

'I remember watching shows when I was little and dreaming about being on stage ... I want to be that for somebody else.'

Lady Gaga

both became famous after dying their hair blonde. You can add to that a joint fearless determination to succeed and a penchant for controversy.

The debate has also spilled over into their music, particularly since the comparisons between 'Born This Way' and Madonna's 'Express Yourself' caused fan websites to hyperventilate. However, the media's desperate attempts to stir up a feud failed. Lady Gaga told US chat show host Jay Leno that she had got an email from Madonna's people 'sending me their love and complete support on behalf of the single'. She continued, 'And if the queen says it shall be then it shall be.'

Wanna Be Startin' Somethin'

When Lady Gaga revealed that she had been asked to support – and duet with – Michael Jackson for some of the London This Is It shows he was working on when he died in 2010, her halo glowed even more brightly for a while. The magic that Jackson created in the recording studio and on stage has left a legacy that is as valid now as it was in the 1980s.

Lady Gaga did not just take her name from Freddie Mercury; his fearless artistic extravagance and vocal style have been a constant inspiration for her. 'Freddie was unique – one of the biggest personalities in the whole of pop music,' she declares. 'He was not only a singer but a fantastic performer, a man of the theater and someone who constantly transformed himself. In short, a genius.'

'It's more *annoying* to me that *people* would *insinuate* that I don't *like* to be compared to *Madonna*.'
Lady Gaga

'He lifted that glittered glove so damn high so his fans could see him, because he was in the art of show business.'

Lady Gaga

The Bitch is Back

She grew up learning to play the piano Elton John's way – and you can still hear the impression that he has left on Lady Gaga. The two of them consummated their mutual admiration at the 2010 Grammies where they performed Elton's 'Your Song' and Gaga's 'Speechless'. They also recorded 'Hello Hello' for the Disney animation *Gnomeo & Juliet* (2011).

Britney Spears is regularly cited as an influence by Gaga for her contagious pop songs and vocal style. Gaga wrote 'Quicksand' for Britney that showed up on *Circus* (2008) and apparently planned to offer her 'Telephone' before it ended up on her 2009 EP *The Fame Monster*.

Feisty 1970s diva Grace Jones is admired by Gaga for her loud costumes and matching stage act. However, she turned down the chance to work with Gaga, saying 'I'd prefer to work with someone who is not copying me'. Smart career move, Grace.

'"Born This Way" is the anthem that's going to obliterate "I Will Survive".'

Sir Elton John

The Girl From New York City

Stefani Joanne Angelina Germanotta was born in Yonkers, a suburb of New York, on 28 March 1986. Her father was an internet entrepreneur and her mother worked full-time as a telecommunications assistant. By the age of four she was singing along to the hits of Michael Jackson and Cyndi Lauper on a cheap plastic cassette player. When she was seven, the family, which now included her one-year-old sister Natali, moved to the more affluent Upper West Side of Manhattan.

At the age of 11 she went to the private, all-girl Convent of the Sacred Heart on Manhattan's Upper East Side. Interestingly it was the same school attended by another of this century's more extrovert females, Paris Hilton. 'I was always the kind of girl who didn't have to listen in class, but would always ace the test and get wasted later with friends,' Lady Gaga says.

Parental Control Advisory

Although she had a relatively privileged upbringing, Lady Gaga dismisses the idea that her parents were affluent. 'They both came from working class families so we've worked for everything – my mother worked eight-to-eight out of the house [in telecommunications], and so did my father. I come from this hustling background so for me it was normal to do it this way.'

She credits her father's wild youth for her own unconventional behaviour, even as she was growing up. She says, 'He saw a lot of himself in me.' However, at the age of 14, when she wanted to try out for auditions in bars, it was her mother who went with her, and it is her mother who has joined her at times on her world tours, keeping her grounded when the pressures of touring threaten to overwhelm her.

'I guess you could say that I'm a bit of a fame Robin Hood. I want young people to know that they can be exactly who they want to be. There is an art to fame.'

Lady Gaga

'I'm blind so I can't really see all those sexy outfits. I can only see her legs when she's on TV. So it's good that she wears those outfits so I can spot her.' Angelin Germanotta, Lady Gaga's grandmother

Early Musical Steps

After learning to pick out her favourite pop songs on her grandmother's piano at the age of five, Stefani's father arranged for her to have piano lessons. Her musical tastes soon broadened out to include 1960s hits of The Beatles and The Rolling Stones. She wrote her first song, a ballad, when she was 13 years old. The following year she began auditioning to appear at open-mic nights at various clubs.

At high school she took leading roles in musical productions such as *Guys And Dolls* and *A Funny Thing Happened To Me On The Way To The Forum*. In 2001, when she was 15 years old, she landed a brief cameo role in an episode of *The Sopranos*. A couple of years later she unwittingly took part in a hidden-camera TV show, but her contribution was edited out when she swore at the 'waitress' who brought her a soiled salad.

The Art School Dance

Finishing high school in 2005 and with her artistic senses already sharpened, Stefani applied to the Tische School of the Arts, part of New York University. She was accepted a year earlier than usual to study drama and performance. During her first year she wrote a thesis on photographer Spencer Tunick, who specializes in photographing large groups of nude people in outdoor locations, and young British artist

'My first piano teacher was a stripper. My dad told me later I used to say to her, "Why do you have such long nails?" She just said, "One day you'll understand".'

Lady Gaga

Damien Hirst, best known for exhibiting dead and dissected animals in formaldehyde in the 1990s.

She was also joining and forming bands while living in a student dormitory on 11th Street and after her first year at the Tische School she decided to take a break from her course and focus on her musical career. Her father agreed to support her on the condition that she would resume her studies if things did not work out.

'Well my music was different in high school. I was singing about love - you know, things I don't care about anymore.'

Lady Gaga

'I had this dream and I really wanted to be a star. I was almost a monster in the way that I was fearless with my ambitions.'

Lady Gaga

Making Career Moves

Moving into an apartment on Rivington Street in New York's bohemian Lower East Side in the summer of 2005, Stefani set about forming a band with local musicians. The less-than-snappily named Stefani Germanotta Band – also known as the SGBand – began rehearsing and recording a five-track demo. 'We used to rehearse at a dingy practice space beneath some grocery store that you'd have to enter through these metal doors on the sidewalk,' remembers guitarist Calvin Pia. 'And she had this huge keyboard that she'd wheel down the street from her apartment.'

They started gigging early in 2006 at the nearby Bitter End Club, selling copies of their demo and an EP they recorded that spring called *Red And Blue*. On stage they played mostly original material, although they slipped in a cover of Led Zeppelin's reggae-ish 'D'yer Mak'er'.

Desperately Seeking Wendy

Stefani's first big break came when the Stefani Germanotta Band played a songwriters showcase gig at the Cutting Room in June 2006 and were spotted by talent scout Wendy Starland who immediately contacted her boss.

'Wendy Starland changed my life.'

Lady Gaga

'I loved what we were doing but it wasn't going to be an easy sell.'

Rob Fusari

'Rob Fusari, a multi-platinum record producer who'd worked with Beyoncé and Jessica Simpson asked me to find him a new girl singer. He wanted somebody edgy, who wouldn't have been out of place in The Strokes,' says Wendy. 'Her band was awful in my opinion. They were college boys and she seemed to be modeling herself after Fiona Apple. Yet when Stefani started singing I was hooked. She had incredible confidence. She carried the audience even though in my opinion the songs were bad. I grabbed hold of her afterwards and said I was going to "change her life".'

And she did.

Musical Makeover

Rob Fusari was not best impressed when Wendy Starland rang him in the middle of the night to enthuse about her new discovery. His mood did not improve when Stefani turned up for an audition. 'She was a little overweight. She had on leggings and some strange cut-up shirt, a hat that looked like it was out of Prince's "Purple Rain".' However, before Stefani had finished singing, Fusari was on the phone to his management, getting them to draw up a contract.

Fusari and Starland set to work, improving Stefani's music and her image. Fusari persuaded her to drop the rock riffs and add dance beats to her songs. Together they co-wrote three songs that would eventually turn up on her first album: 'Paparazzi', 'Beautiful, Dirty, Rich' and 'Again Again'. For a while their relationship was personal as well as professional.

Introducing ...
Lady Gaga

No one is sure when Stefani Germanotta changed her name to Lady Gaga. However, no one doubts that Queen's 1984 hit 'Radio Gaga' was the inspiration. The song was a favourite of Rob Fusari. 'Every day when Stef came into the studio, instead of saying hello I would start singing "Radio Gaga".' He says the name arose after a texting error: 'I typed Radio Gaga and it did an autocorrect so somehow "Radio" got changed to "Lady".' She texted back, 'That's it.' 'After that day she was Lady Gaga. She's like "Don't ever call me Stefani again".'

However, Wendy Starland says that the name came out of a brainstorming meeting before they started shopping around the record labels. And Lady Gaga herself said in an interview in 2009 that her 'realization of Gaga was five years ago, but Gaga's always been who I am'.

'Gaga's always been who I am.'
Lady Gaga

Movers And Shakers

The first record company to show an interest in Lady Gaga was Def Jam, the hip-hop and urban music label. When head honcho LA Reid walked in during the audition and started drumming his fingers to the beat on a table, the deal was effectively done. She signed a contract in September 2006 with a reported advance of $850,000 and plans to release an album the following summer.

But three months later the contract was terminated without explanation. 'She couldn't even talk when she told me because she was crying so hard,' remembers Rob Fusari. But through her tears, Lady Gaga was smart enough to waive part of her advance in exchange for ownership of the master tapes she'd already produced – which contained two future hits. 'I went back to my apartment and I was so depressed. That's when I started the real devotion to my music and art,' she said.

'LA told me I was a star.'

Lady Gaga

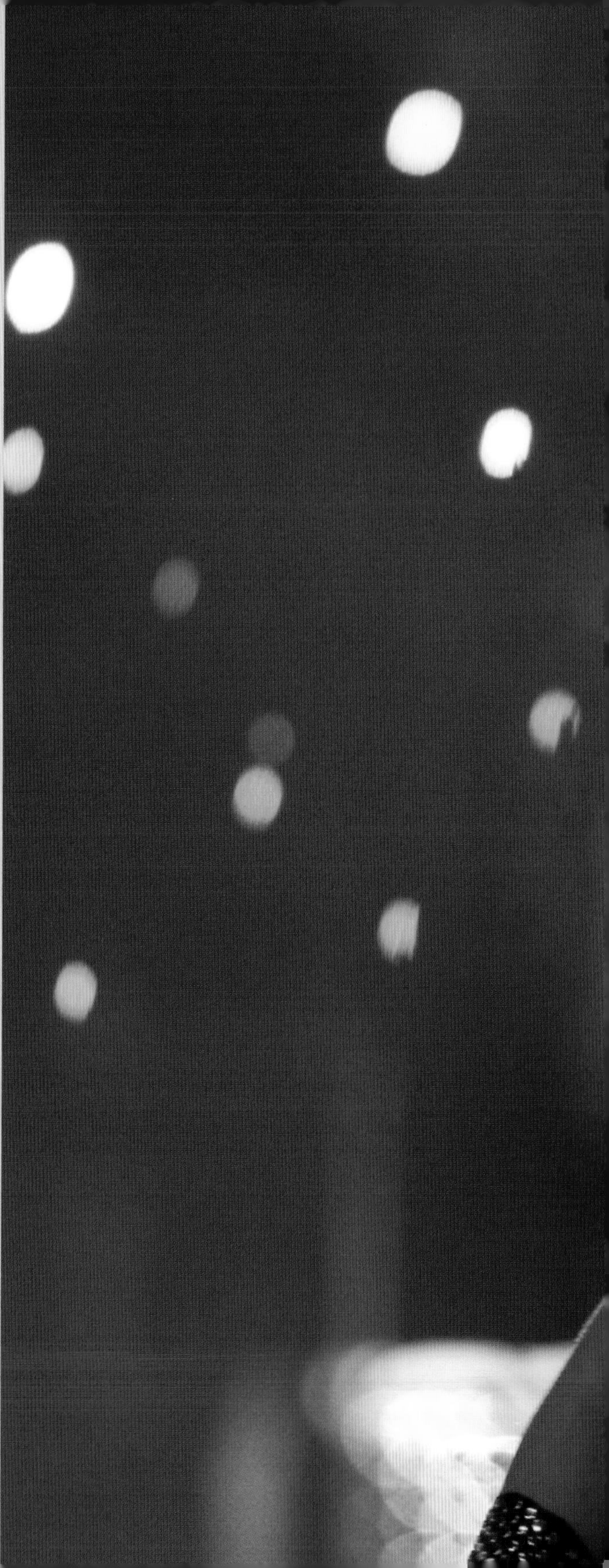

Starlight Burlesque

Lady Gaga drowned her sorrows in the unfashionable glam-rock/art trash scene where she encountered performance artist Lady Starlight who introduced her to the joys of burlesque and go-go dancing. Together they formed Lady Gaga & The Starlight Revue with Gaga in little more than a bikini playing synthesizers and Starlight spinning beats as they danced to choreographed go-go moves beneath shiny disco balls and set alight jets of hairspray.

They had a weekly club 'party' and also appeared at the prestigious indie rock festival Lollapalooza in Chicago. While Gaga was safe enough in her underwear on stage, she ran into trouble with local cops as she wandered around the festival site. Gaga has admitted that drugs were consumed during this period. She also acquired a boyfriend, heavy metal drummer and bar manager Luc Carl.

Relaunch

Rob Fusari kept a low profile during Lady Gaga's burlesque phase but he continued hustling on her behalf, and when his producer friend Vincent Herbert landed a licensing deal for his Streamline label with Interscope Records in spring 2007, he was quick off the mark. Vincent had written and produced hits for Destiny's Child, Michael Jackson and Stevie Wonder and was looking for new acts to sign.

Fusari called Herbert in Los Angeles and told him to check out Lady Gaga's Facebook page. Herbert rang back the same day

'Starlight and I bonded *instantly* over her love of **heavy metal** and my love of **boys** that listen to **heavy metal.**'

Lady Gaga

'I really feel that *Vincent Herbert* and I made pop history and we're going to keep on doing it.'

Lady Gaga

to arrange a meeting with Interscope boss Jimmy Iovine. 'He listens to a little bit of "Beautiful, Dirty, Rich" and to another record Stef and I did called "Sexy Ugly",' recalls Fusari. 'He stands up, looks at Vince and says "Let's give it a try".'

Gearing Up For Fame

Lady Gaga was initially set up as a songwriter for The Pussycat Dolls and Britney Spears (who was in the midst of her public meltdown) while recording her own tracks with Moroccan/Swedish producer RedOne who had extensive knowledge of the British and European dance scene. She continued to focus on her image, as did Vincent Herbert. When someone in the audience at Lollapalooza shouted 'Amy Winehouse', Herbert advised her to go blonde. 'She did it right away. God bless that girl, she really does listen.'

Everything clicked into place when Gaga recorded 'Just Dance'. Her songwriting took a leap forward and RedOne's speedy beats and synthi-pop sounds had a global appeal. When Senegalese R&B singer Akon, an international star, heard the song he was mad for it. Suddenly the lights went on around Interscope Records. Lady Gaga found herself working with a choreographer on moves to match the music.

'*Gaga* and I believe the world needs this music, that it is a *way* to unite.'

Producer RedOne

Fame Is A-Coming...

In late 2007 Lady Gaga relocated from New York to Los Angeles to complete the tracks on her first album, working closely with Interscope Records. Her producer, RedOne, who had previously worked on Kat Deluna's solo album, *9 Lives*, skilfully mixed Gaga's eclectic range of styles – from glam rock to metal – into a synthesizer-heavy R&B tainted dance-pop with urgent beats. His extensive knowledge of Europop, a genre not widely known in America, ensured that virtually every track featured an addictive melody or hook.

Gaga also brought with her the three songs she had written and recorded with Rob Fusari in New York and used Interscope's A&R chief Martin Kierszenbaum as co-writer and producer on a couple of tracks, as well as the writing and production team of Brian Kierulf and Josh Schwarz, best known for their work with Britney Spears.

Hits From The Fame

Just as *The Fame* came out in August 2008, the first single, 'Just Dance', was starting to climb the US charts. Written with RedOne and Gaga's mentor, Akon, 'Just Dance' featured another of Akon's protégés, pop/R&B singer Colby O'Donis. Released some four months earlier, it had been a club and

'I'm defying all the preconceptions we have of pop artists.'

Lady Gaga

dancefloor hit over the summer. It finally made No. 1 in January 2009 – around the same time it topped the UK charts – sparking a resurgence of *The Fame* album, which peaked at No. 4 in March.

In contrast, the second single, the innuendo-laden 'Poker Face' (co-written with RedOne), took less than a month to hit the US top spot. Over the summer of 2009 the song went globally viral, eventually selling over 9 million copies. From this point on, Lady Gaga was impossible to ignore.

'Everyone was telling me I wasn't pop last year, and now look - so don't tell me what pop is. I know what pop is.'
Lady Gaga

The Fame Monster

Originally planned as a bonus disc for a deluxe edition of *The Fame*, Lady Gaga decided to release the eight-track EP *The Fame Monster* as a standalone CD in November 2009 – in the US at least. Both versions charted in the first week; at No. 5 and 6 respectively. In the UK the deluxe edition sent *The Fame* back to the top of the charts.

The songs were written while Gaga was travelling the world on her Fame Tour and deliberately focus on a darker, contrasting mood to *The Fame*. According to Gaga herself: 'I spent a lot of nights in Eastern Europe and this album is a pop experimentation with industrial/goth beats, 90s dance melodies, an obsession with the lyrical genius of 80s melodic pop and the runway. I wrote while watching muted fashion shows and I am compelled to say my music was scored for them.'

Monster Hits

The first single from *The Fame Monster*, 'Bad Romance', was hailed as Lady Gaga's best yet and proof that she was more than a one-hit wonder. Another Gaga/RedOne collaboration, 'Bad Romance' peaked at No. 2 in the US. In the UK it topped the charts in December 2009, making Gaga the first lady to have three British No. 1 hits in a year.

The second single, 'Telephone', was originally written for Britney Spears, but was rejected by her label. It was co-written by Rodney Jenkins, who has worked with Jennifer Lopez, Michael Jackson and Beyoncé. He makes a guest appearance in the middle of the song, which is about preferring to dance rather than answer her boyfriend's call. A third single, 'Alejandro', was a return to Europop territory with a Latin slant, keeping her on the airwaves for the second successive summer.

'While traveling the world I've encountered several monsters, each represented by a different song on the new record.'
Lady Gaga

'Some *artists* want your **money** so they can buy Range Rovers and *diamond* bracelets, but I don't **care** about that kind of **stuff.** I want your **soul.**'

Lady Gaga

It's All In The Mix

A remix album of Lady Gaga's biggest hits was inevitable, given the incredible success she had enjoyed with *The Fame* and *The Fame Monster*. *The Remix* (2010) was initially released in Japan in March 2010, selling more than 250,000 copies. A revised edition of the album came out in the rest of the world during the summer of 2010 and sales have passed half a million, making it one of the top ten bestselling remix albums.

The remixes, which were already individually available on various single formats, include The Pet Shop Boys ('Eh Eh [Nothing Else I Can Say]'), Passion Pit ('Telephone'), The Sound Of Arrows ('Alejandro'), Chew Fu featuring Marilyn Manson ('LoveGame'), Stuart Price ('Paparazzi') and Richard Vission ('Just Dance'), as well as an acoustic piano/vocal version of 'Poker Face'. The album was also a reflection of Gaga's impact on the dance scene.

'She's a great musician, she's a great singer, and she's laughing when she's doing it, the same way that I am.'

Marilyn Manson

Born This Way

Lady Gaga started working on her second 'proper' album, *Born This Way*, in the spring of 2010 and recorded the songs at various studios around the world during her relentless touring schedule. These included London's Abbey Road, Gang Studios in Paris, Mechaniche in Milan, Livingroom in Oslo and studios in Australia, New York, Miami and Las Vegas.

She was not just broadening out geographically but musically. Gaga's influences now included new wave, mainstream rock and opera, and the synthesizers sometimes gave way to electric guitars and violins. Guest appearances on the album included Queen guitarist Brian May and saxophonist Clarence Clemons from Bruce Springsteen's East Street Band (who died less than a month after the album was released in May 2011). While she co-wrote and produced every track, Gaga also enlisted new producers and writers such as Fernando Garibay, Jeppe Laursen, DJ White Shadow and Robert 'Mutt' Lange. Only RedOne remained from her earlier albums.

Born Controversial

The first two singles from the *Born This Way* album sparked condemnation from religious groups and even some governments. Lady Gaga's strong stance on sexuality and feminism on the album's title song was deemed 'immoral' by fundamentalist Christian and Islamic organizations, while the references to Mary Magdalene in the second single, 'Judas',

'It includes the greatest music I've ever written.'

Lady Gaga

'Don't be a drag, just be a queen.'

Lyrics from 'Born This Way'

provoked anger from the Catholic Church. Radio stations in Malaysia were ordered to edit the lyrics of 'Born This Way' by the government. And 'Judas' was banned in Lebanon after protests from the Catholic Information Centre – the government even temporarily banned the *Born This Way* album.

None of this harmed the commercial success of the album or singles. The 'Born This Way' single sold over a million copies worldwide in its first week of release, while the album topped 1.5 million sales.

Digital Domination

No one has taken more advantage of the digital era than Lady Gaga, who has become the first artist to sell more than 20 million single downloads. Her first single, 'Just Dance', sold over 6 million digital copies, while the 'Born This Way' single is the fastest-selling single in iTunes history. In addition, people have listened to her songs on free streams on YouTube and other online services literally hundreds of millions of times – her myspace site alone has had over 400 million plays.

Gaga's digital album sales highlight the rapid growth of the market. While US digital sales of *The Fame* have topped a million, *Born This Way* had digital sales of more than 600,000 in its first week. Amazon accounted for some 440,000 sales with a two-day promotional campaign offering the album for 99 cents, a marketing ploy that cost the company over $3 million.

'I'm just trying to change the world, one sequin at a time.'
Lady Gaga

'When I'm writing music I'm thinking about the clothes I want to wear on stage. It's all about everything altogether - performance art, pop performance art, fashion.'

Lady Gaga

Putting On The Style

From the start Lady Gaga has indulged her outrageous fashion sense. From her tea-party sunglasses to her Ice-Lady disco stick, Gaga has encouraged her fans to expect the unexpected. Many of her most eccentric outfits are known by their nicknames – the meat dress, the Kermit dress, the bubble dress, the red veil.

It is no coincidence that she has worn some of her most memorable costumes at the MTV Video Awards. In 2009 she arrived in a black-feathered Victorian gown with a gold *Phantom Of The Opera* mask. In 2010 she wore her famous meat dress as a personal and political statement, although animal rights groups still managed to be offended. In 2011 Gaga turned up for a *Good Morning America* TV show interview in a latex sheath dress, deliberately reminiscent of a condom, as she was promoting HIV and AIDS awareness.

Baby Let's Play Haus

To help realize her visions of fashion and style, Lady Gaga set up the Haus Of Gaga in 2008, a creative team to work on her costumes and stage designs. The Haus was funded by Gaga's songwriting royalties and she was able to put her own team

together. 'I called up all my coolest friends and we sat in a room and I said that I wanted to make my face light up. Or that I wanted to make a pair of dope sunglasses. Or that I wanted to make video glasses. Or whatever it was that I wanted to do.'

The Haus Of Gaga has always been a loose-knit team and has expanded along with Gaga's career. It includes the dogs who have made brief cameo appearances in virtually all Gaga's videos. Outside human designers and artists are brought in to work on specific projects.

The Power Of Videos

Lady Gaga's hyperactive sense of imagery has ensured that her videos are as memorable as the singles they promote. She has teamed up with a variety of directors to spectacular effect, reviving the video medium on terrestrial television and exploiting the free-stream services on the internet, reaching her fan base on demand.

Early videos established Gaga's own image. About 'Just Dance', she says, 'It's really me, it's like, this is my life! I'm not doing a video in a nightclub. I'm doing a house party in Brooklyn. That's what I know.' For 'Poker Face' she says, 'I knew I wanted it to be sexy so I thought "no pants", because that's sexy. And I knew I wanted it to be futuristic so I thought "shoulder pads" because that's my thing.' The imagery became more extreme on 'LoveGame', provoking controversy with sexually suggestive movements and bondage.

'I didn't want a condo or a car because I don't drive and I'm never f***ing home, so I just wanted to put all my money into the performance.'

Lady Gaga

'A girl's got to use what she's given and I'm not going to make a guy drool the way a Britney video does.'

Lady Gaga

More Videos, More Power

The videos from *The Fame Monster* continued to raise controversy. Lady Gaga and Beyoncé's homage to Quentin Tarantino's movie *Kill Bill* (2003–2004) for the 'Telephone' promo brought criticism for the amount of skin on display, the lesbian relationship and the 'mass homicide'. The video was given an 18-restriction on YouTube. The homoerotic scenes in 'Alejandro' also upset the moral guardians, and the Catholic League was outraged by Gaga devouring a set of rosary beads.

But Gaga made no attempt to tone down her message. Images of her giving birth to a new prejudice-free race on 'Born This Way' were guaranteed to offend some people, as were the scenes of Jesus, Judas and Mary Magdalene riding into the 'new' Jerusalem on motorbikes in the 'Judas' video. However, she ditched the religious references and the kinky sex for the 1980s-styled 'Edge Of Glory'. And there were only a few scratches on the love-seeking 'Yoü And I'.

'I take it to extremes. It's meant to make guys think "I don't know if this is sexy or just weird".'

Lady Gaga

Tour De Force

Lady Gaga got her first opportunity to put her concert show together when she landed the support slot on the reformed New Kids On The Block 27-date American tour in September 2008. The set, designed by the Haus Of Gaga, featured a table for DJ Space Cowboy and three mobile LCD screens showing specially made videos. Gaga wore a white origami dress and special Haus headset and was backed by four male dancers on stage.

She followed that tour early in 2009 with another support slot for The Pussycat Dolls on the European and Australian legs of their Doll Domination Tour. She had a backdrop of an urban scene that featured high-rise buildings, city lights, smoke stacks that emitted real smoke and illuminated billboards including one for The Fame Machine. Other stage effects were created using a special translucent screen and dramatic lighting.

'Well, you know I love a girl in her underwear, first of all. Secondly, I've been writing for them.'
Lady Gaga on The Pussycat Dolls

Having A Ball

For her first headlining tour Lady Gaga was able to make use of the entire stage area and wasted no time in filling it up. Three versions of the show were prepared, depending on the size of the venue. She says, 'It's not really a tour, more of a traveling party, as if you're walking into New York circa 1974. There's an art installation in the lobby, a DJ spinning your favorite records and then the most haunting performance that you've ever seen on the stage.'

The Fame Ball Tour criss-crossed the US between March and May 2009 before Gaga headed off to Australia with The Pussycat Dolls. For the second leg, which toured around Europe from June to September, Gaga was finally able to use a live band consisting of musician friends from New York, as well as updating her costumes.

Unleashing The Monster

The Monster Ball Tour was put together in late 2009 after a planned tour with Kanye West fell through. The aim was to create a 'pop-electro opera' show that was creative and expensive-looking but affordable to her fast-growing fan base. The theme was evolution, reflecting the changes Gaga had been through recording her *Fame Monster* album.

The first leg of the tour ran from November 2009 to January 2010, playing theatres in the US. The advance demand for tickets was so great that the tour was upgraded from theatres

'Hang it!
Hang everything!
Find a place to hang it!
That's my motto.'

Lady Gaga

'It's the greatest post-apocalyptic house party that you've ever been to.'

Lady Gaga

to arenas and the show was redesigned accordingly. The Monster Ball Tour resumed in the UK in February 2010 and ran for the next 15 months, mainly around Europe and the US but also taking in Australia and finishing up in Mexico City 106 shows later – one of the highest-grossing tours of all time.

Born To Tour

Having set up a series of 'Haus parties' to promote the release of her *Born This Way* album, Lady Gaga revealed that her Born This Way Tour would start in 2012, although she promised some one-off shows before then. Just as her Monster Ball Tour was extensive, the Born This Way Tour will take in South America, India and Indonesia as well as the US, Europe and Australia.

With dates still to be announced, Gaga was already tweeting: 'I love Monsterball. Can't wait for the next tour. I know exactly what I want it to look and feel like, down to every detail.' She also revealed that the set list for the show will include 'Heavy Metal Lover', 'Poker Face', 'Just Dance', 'Paparazzi', 'Dance In The Dark' and 'LoveGame'.

'We did a theater in an arena and it worked. How do we take it to the next level?'

Laurieann Gibson, Lady Gaga's creative director

A Social Whirl

Lady Gaga has voraciously used social networking and free-stream sites to promote her career. She tops the Social 50, a chart that measures how popular people are on social media sites, including Facebook, Twitter and YouTube.

In July 2010 Gaga became the first living person to have 10 million followers on Facebook. A year later that figure had swollen to 40 million, although she was now facing competition from Rihanna and Justin Bieber. Part of the reason for Gaga's appeal on Facebook is that she is both active and responsive. To her followers she keeps it real and does not indulge in the kind of desperate publicity stunts that blight some other artists. She has collaborated with Zynga, the company that makes online games for Facebook, both to promote her records and also to raise money for the Japanese 2011 earthquake/tsunami victims.

'Remember that your career will never wake up and tell you that it doesn't love you anymore.' Lady Gaga

> *'Ten million monsters!*
> *I'm speechless, we did it.*
> *It's an illness how*
> *I love you.'*
>
> Lady Gaga

Googled And Twittered

Type 'Lady Gaga' into Google and there will be more than 600 million results. Gaga herself has admitted that even she Googles herself. When she visited Google's headquarters in Mountain View, California, for a meet-and-greet with staff and an interview for YouTube, she was welcomed with a Google Trends video that featured an image of her built from words in her tag cloud.

Gaga had understandably been asked not to advertie her Google visit, but when she Googled herself afterwards and failed to find much, she tweeted about it on her Twitter site and immediately increased the audience for the YouTube interview dramatically. The first person to accumulate 10 million followers on Twitter in the spring of 2011, that figure had already grown to 12 million by the autumn. She used her followers to raise $1 million on World AIDS Day in November 2010.

Quicker By YouTube

While the record business remains paranoid about free-streaming sites such as YouTube, Lady Gaga realizes that it is the fastest way to get her musical and visual messages across to her fans. She has had over a billion hits on the site and has set up her own official channel.

Gaga uses her channel not just for her official music videos but also to keep her followers closely engaged, such as the clip from a Toronto concert when she invited 10-year-old

'I am focused on the work. I am constantly creating. I live and breathe my work. I love my work. There's no stopping. I didn't create the fame, the fame created me.'

Lady Gaga

Maria Aragon, whose cover of 'Born This Way' had recently gone viral on YouTube, to join her on stage. They sang the song in front of 20,000 people and Gaga's eyes welled with tears as Maria gave a shoutout to her family and friends in Winnipeg, Canada. It was a genuine YouTube moment.

'To really love someone you have to share your art with them.'

Lady Gaga

Taking Social Control

Not surprisingly, Lady Gaga has been making plans to create her own social network. Together with Google she is helping to fund a new site – so far unnamed but possibly to be called Backplane – aimed at online communities with specific interests, such as music and sport. Gaga's manager, Troy Carter, says that these specialist communities 'need a more concentrated base for them to socialize'. It will also integrate updates from Facebook, Twitter and other social-networking sites to provide a comprehensive coverage for entertainment and sports fans.

Meanwhile, Gaga continues to make her Gagavision transmissions – a series of blogs about her wardrobe, fashion, Haus Of Gaga designs, touring and recording plans, celebrities, other artists and fan videos. It is available on as many sites and formats as possible, including the iPhone and iPad Touch.

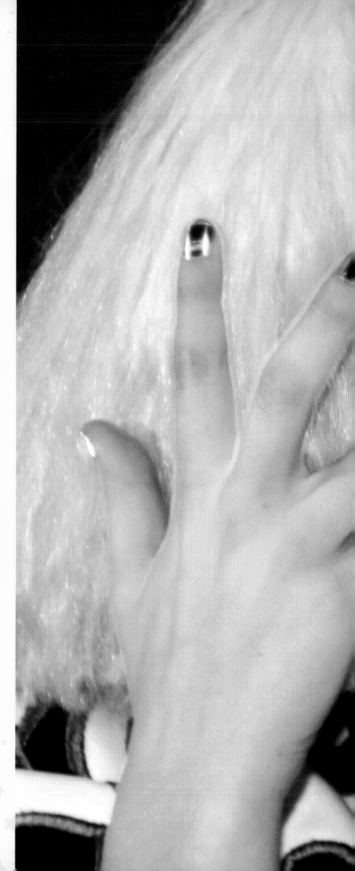

The Lady Gaga Effect

Lady Gaga is not just a digital queen, she reigns supreme over the traditional media scene too. Nobody knows the power of Gaga better than a magazine editor. She has appeared on over 100 magazine covers and all of them experienced a circulation surge as a result. This was particularly true in 2010, the year of Gaga-mania in the media. *Rolling Stone* and *Cosmopolitan* both scored their biggest-selling issues of the year with their Gaga covers. Only Angelina Jolie was able to pull in more readers at *Vanity Fair*.

The covers were invariably flamboyant but not risqué, except for the British *Q* magazine, which was banned in the US for displaying the lower portion of one breast – an infringement of New York State law. How the moral guardians missed the strap-on dildo beneath Gaga's trousers remains a mystery.

'Don't you think that what's on the cover of a magazine is quite artificial?'

Lady Gaga

'For me, more than *anything*, I want to do *something* important. It's *gotta* be important. If it's coming out of my *mouth*, if it's going on my *body*, if it's going on *TV*, it better be *important*.'

Lady Gaga

Small-screen Heroine

Television brought Lady Gaga's wacky image into sitting rooms across the world. During 2009, as *The Fame* and singles increasingly dominated the charts, she made over 60 TV appearances in the US, UK, Japan, Australia, Germany, France, Italy, Spain and even Malta.

Since then Gaga has been more selective but no less effective. Apart from award shows and guest performances, she has used chat shows to get over a message to go with the image. And she generally leaves at least one good quote behind to be picked up by the gossip columns. Even a Korean news programme got exclusive details of the upcoming *Born This Way* album. Her success has inevitably been referenced in other TV shows, notably *Glee*, which has devoted two episodes to her songs. The parody of Poker Face' in *South Park* was a different kind of accolade.

The 3D Screen

The Super-Deluxe edition of *The Fame Monster* released in December 2009 included a pair of 3-D glasses 'for things that will happen soon'. In March 2010 Lady Gaga tweeted that 'the Monster Ball DVD is going to be released and it will be in 3D!' However, there was no further news until February 2011 when Gaga told TV chat-show host Jay Leno she was filming her New York Madison Square Garden concerts that month for an HBO television special that aired in May – but not in 3D. More news on the DVD is awaited.

'I'm working on bringing the instant film camera back as part of the future.'

Lady Gaga

Meanwhile, Gaga's 3D activities have been restricted to her fingernails – picking up on the 3D nail fashion that started in Japan with girls decorating their extended nails with gels, glitter, figurines and flowers. Gaga has been seen with jewellery and tiny boxes on her nails.

The Silver Screen

Although Lady Gaga has given no indication of any movie plans, that has not stopped the media from speculating. In August 2010 (traditionally a slow month for real news), UK tabloid *News Of The World* reported that Gaga was in discussions to make a 'blockbuster' movie, pitched somewhere between Michael Jackson's *Moonwalker* (1988) and Beyonce's role in *Dreamgirls* (2006). There was even a director lined up, Bryan Singer, who directed *The Usual Suspects* (1995) and *X-Men* (2000). Gaga's office denied the story.

Exactly a year later, more stories claimed that Gaga was in 'secret discussions' to play Amy Winehouse in a biopic of the late singer's life. Although Gaga has expressed her admiration for Winehouse, the rest appears to be Hollywood gossip. Gaga did express, however, if making a biopic of her life, she would like Marisa Tomei to play her part.

'If only my fans knew I was peeing in a beer cup backstage.' Lady Gaga

All We Need Is Lady Gaga

It took little more than a year for Lady Gaga to be transformed from an ex-burlesque dancer to a global pop star. Within another two years she had risen from a star to an icon. There was clearly a pent-up demand for a star like Gaga that transcended her natural talents as a singer, songwriter and performer.

A large part of her appeal is down to her relatively normal upbringing. She grew up exposed to pop culture in the same way as most of her generation. She was not a child star who was relentlessly pushed into the spotlight before she properly understood what was happening to her. Gaga knew exactly what was happening to her. She had consumed pop culture voraciously from an early age. She understood her audience because, as Stefani Germanotta, she had been one of them.

From Germanotta To Gaga

The transition from Stefani Germanotta to Lady Gaga was seamless, because she had been creating her alter ego in her head for several years before it actually happened. Her first producer, Rob Fusari, who introduced her to Interscope Records and was also, briefly, her boyfriend, remembers that

she used to carry around a scrapbook of things that inspired her – music, fashion, visual ideas, even everyday items that she saw around her.

'She would show me the scrapbook every once in a while,' recalls Fusari, 'and to me it meant very little, but I feel it was her way of finding building blocks that she could use to formulate how she wanted the world to see Lady Gaga.' He continued, 'Now, if only fans could get their hands on that scrapbook they'd really be able to understand her.'

'Love is like a brick.
You can build a house or
you can sink a dead body.'
Lady Gaga

Gaga's Little Monsters

The special relationship that Lady Gaga has built up with her fans has given her an intensely loyal following. From the beginning she encouraged her fans to follow her on Facebook and Twitter where she posted messages to them. She started referring to them as 'little monsters' – and to herself as

'mother monster' – before the release of *The Fame Monster* that included a Manifesto of Little Monsters in the Book of Gaga that came with the Super-Deluxe edition.

Gaga invariably credits her little monsters with her successes at awards shows and posted the lyrics of 'Born This Way' for them a few days before the single's release. In February 2011, she added to her collection of tattoos with one dedicated to her little monsters. 'Look what I did last night,' she tweeted. 'Little Monsters forever. On the arm that holds my mic.'

From Gaga To Calderone

In August 2011, at the MTV Video Music Awards, Lady Gaga publicly introduced her new alter-ego, Jo Calderone, who had made a cameo appearance in the 'Yoü And I' video. Wearing a loose black suit with black slicked-back hair and holding a cigarette, Jo sauntered on stage and started talking about his relationship with Lady Gaga. 'She left me. She said it always starts out good … She said I'm just like the last one.' Jo then sat at the piano and started playing 'Yoü And I'. When Queen guitarist Brian May appeared on stage for his solo, Jo leapt up on the piano and sprayed the audience with beer.

Afterwards, Gaga spoke about whether Jo would return to the spotlight. 'I don't know how soon, but I'm sure Jo will want to perform again,' she said. 'I don't think he can help himself, really.'

'I'm interested in all the different people we can become or have become in the past.'
Lady Gaga

Fame Versus Privacy

Lady Gaga effectively gave up her private life when she signed her record deal with Interscope. Since *The Fame* was released, she has lived her life as Lady Gaga in the public eye 24/7. She chose to put her professional life ahead of her personal life, saying that music cannot disappoint her, 'unlike men'. This explains her dedication to her 'little monsters', whose unequivocal love she cherishes. No wonder she says 'to really love someone you have to share your art with them'.

While she seems at ease discussing any aspect of her life in public, Gaga admits that she lies to protect a certain degree of privacy. 'I believe as an artist that being private in public is at the core of the esthetic, the message. However, I profusely lie about my personal relationships in an effort to protect that esthetic, that message.'

Giving It Back

Since Lady Gaga became successful in 2009 she has used her influence to support her chosen causes and campaigns. Some have been a response to natural disasters, such as the 2010 Haitian earthquake and the 2011 Japanese earthquake and tsunami. Other causes reflect her personal beliefs. Having

> 'I do sometimes feel that I'm on stage all the time, and I do feel that life is a stage for my art – when I'm dancing, singing, making breakfast.'
>
> Lady Gaga

> *'You put your lipstick on and you bring a condom out with you. There are no exceptions.'*
>
> *Lady Gaga*

declared her bisexuality in 2009 and in acknowledgement of her large gay following, she launched Viva Glam Gaga lipstick, with proceeds going to educating women on the risks of HIV and AIDS. She has campaigned for gay rights, appearing at the 2010 MTV Video Music Awards accompanied by four gay members of the American armed forces who had been discriminated against, and at Europride in Rome in 2011 where she criticized the lack of gay rights in many European countries.

She has also supported homeless and children's charities in the US and UK, appearing at ex-president Bill Clinton's homeless fundraiser in October 2011 and the BBC's Children In Need Rocks Manchester in November 2011.

Body Art

A fan of tattoos, Lady Gaga has so far restricted her skin decorations to the left side of her body, apparently because her father asked her to. The tattoos include a peace sign on her wrist; a tribute to her 'little monsters' on her upper arm, next to a quote from her favourite German poet and philosopher Rainer Maria Rilke; a Hawaiian daisy on her shoulder; and a unicorn on her left thigh with the words 'Born This Way' (a phrase she first used at the 2010 MTV Video Music Awards) wrapped around its horn.

The appearance of horn-like ridges on Gaga's cheeks, temples and shoulders in 2011 caused some controversy. She denied that the effect had involved the use of plastic

surgery, to which she is opposed. However, she remained coy about how the effect was actually achieved.

'I am an artist and I have the ability and the free will to choose the way the world will envision me.' Lady Gaga

Bringing Back Polaroid

Lady Gaga may have made full use of new technology, but she is reviving old technology too. The Polaroid camera was a favourite with Gaga when she was growing up and she has always been aware of the Polaroid's unique features. Early in 2010 she was appointed creative director at Polaroid and a year later unveiled a new range of products, the most Gaga-esque of which was a pair of camera sunglasses developed in collaboration with Ammunition, the company that designed the Beats By Dr Dre headphones.

The sunglasses have two embedded LCD displays just below the sightline, enabling you to see normally above them, and a camera situated on the bridge of the nose. It can also be pre-loaded with slideshows and video, but probably not with the leaked Polaroid outtakes of Gaga's raunchy *Vogue* cover session.

'It really came from Gaga - from her video for "Poker Face" with the glasses that say "pop culture". She wanted to build that into a product.'
Robert Brunner, creative director of Ammunition

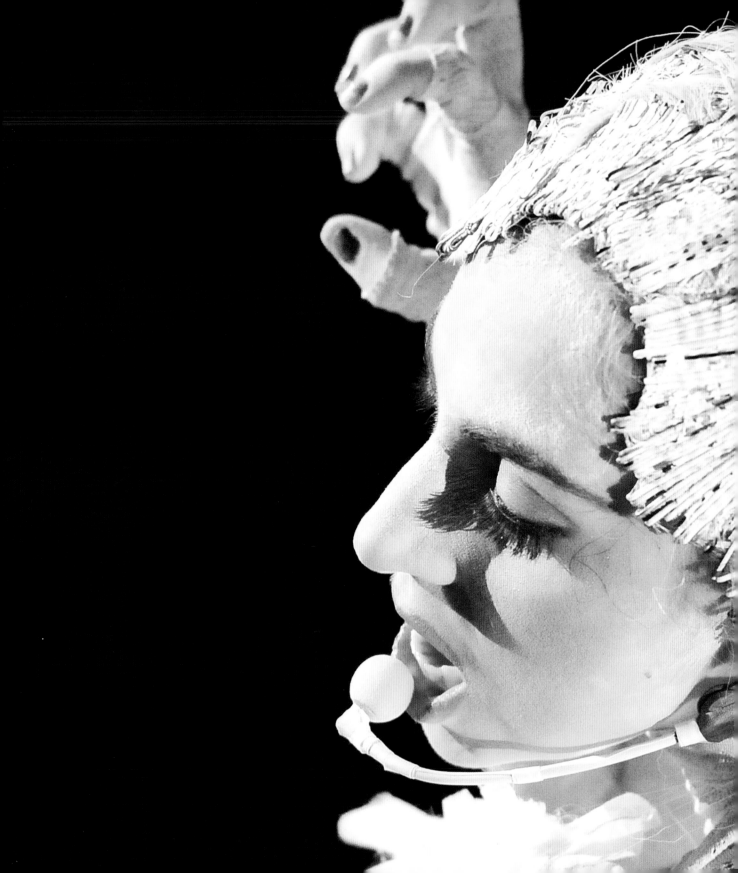

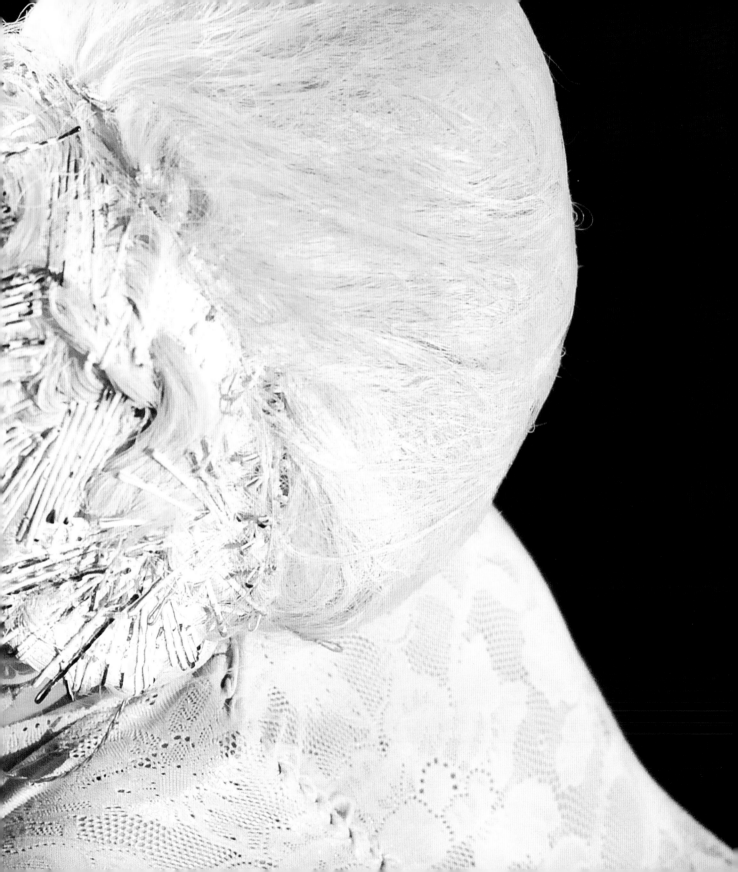

Gaga Trivia

Lady Gaga is the first female artist to score three UK No. 1 hits in one year. She is also the first (and probably only) artist to score a No. 1 hit in the first two decades of the twenty-first century with the same song ('Bad Romance' went to No. 1 in December 2009 and again in January 2010).

Lady Gaga is rarely upstaged, but her appearance at the 2009 American Music Awards was eclipsed by the openly gay *American Idol* winner Adam Lambert, whose performance included simulated oral sex, a guy-on-guy kiss and a giant mirror for the audience to see their own shocked reaction.

Conspiracy theorists are convinced that the lyrics and 'occult symbolism' of the 'Born This Way' video are proof that Lady Gaga is a member of the secret Illuminati society that is planning to establish a new world order by mind control.

And More . . .

Bette Midler was not amused when she heard that Lady Gaga had copied her comedy routine of being pushed around in a wheelchair dressed as a mermaid during her 2010 Australian tour. 'You can keep the meat dress and the firecracker tits, the mermaid's mine,' she tweeted. After Gaga gushed apologies and appreciation, Midler decided that 'fabulous mermaids can co-exist' after all.

'Don't you ever let a soul in the world tell you that you can't be exactly who you are.'
Lady Gaga

A local fish and chip bar got an unexpected order for 35 portions of fish and chips to be delivered to the Cardiff International Arena the night Lady Gaga played the venue in March 2010. 'I had a call to say her crew would like to experience our fish and chips,' said Tariq Siddique, boss of the Albany Fish Bar.

Lady Gaga is 1.55 m (5ft 1 inch) tall.

Lady Gaga is not a hermaphrodite, a transsexual or indeed a male.

The Future Is Gaga

If the second half of 2011 was relatively quiet for Lady Gaga, she will be back in your face in 2012 with a world tour and a new album. Unlike the Monster Ball Tour which was expanded as the demand for tickets spiralled, the new tour will take advantage of large-scale production with spectacular stage designs and effects, as well as a new range of costumes from the Haus Of Gaga.

She has also been recording tracks for her next album, which is likely to come out in spring 2012. And there will be more collaborations such as 'The Greatest Thing', the duet she's done with Cher. Taking a break from recording and rehearsing, Gaga told US radio host Ryan Seacrest that she was 'very excited and busy because I have lots of ideas and I know exactly how I want everything to look'.

'She is perfectly, almost *genetically* engineered to be a twenty-first century *pop star.*'

Eric Garland,
CEO Big Champagne
Media Measurement.

Further Information

Lady Gaga Vital Info

Birth Name   Stefani Joanne Angelina Germanotta

Birth Date   28 March 1986

Birth Place   New York City

Height   1.55 m (5 ft 1 in)

Nationality   American

Hair Colour   Brown; usually dyed platinum blonde

Eye Colour   Hazel

Alter Egos   Lady Gaga, Jo Calderone

Discography

Albums & EPs

The Fame (2008)

The Cherrytree Sessions (EP, 2009)

Hitmixes (EP, 2009)

The Fame Monster (EP, 2009)

The Remix (2010)

The Singles (2010)

Born This Way (2011)

Singles

2008:   'Just Dance' (No. 1)
'Poker Face' (No. 1)

2009:   'Eh, Eh (Nothing Else I Can Say)'
'LoveGame'
'Paparazzi'
'Bad Romance' (No. 1)

2010:   'Telephone' (No. 1, with Beyoncé)
'Alejandro'

2011:   'Born This Way' (No. 1)
'Judas'
'The Edge of Glory'
'Yoü and I'

Awards

American Music Awards

2010:   Favorite Pop/Rock Female Artist

Billboard Music Awards

2011:   Top Pop Artist
Top Dance Artist
Top Electronic/Dance Album *The Fame*

BRIT Awards

2010:   Female Solo Artist
International Breakthrough Act
Best International Album *The Fame*

CFDA Fashion Awards

2011:   Fashion Icon Award

Grammy Awards

2010:   Best Electronic/Dance Album *The Fame*

Best Dance Record 'Poker Face'

2011:   Best Pop Vocal Album *The Fame Monster*

Best Female Pop Vocal Performance 'Bad Romance'

Best Short Form Music Video 'Bad Romance'

MTV Europe Music Awards

2009:   Best New Act

2010:   Best Female

Best Pop

Best Song 'Bad Romance'

MTV Video Music Awards

2009:   Best New Artist 'Poker Face'

Best Special Effects 'Paparazzi'

Best Art Direction 'Paparazzi'

2010:   Video of the Year 'Bad Romance'

Best Female Video 'Bad Romance'

Best Pop Video 'Bad Romance'

Best Dance Video 'Bad Romance'

Best Choreography 'Bad Romance'

Best Collaboration 'Telephone'

2011:   Best Female Video 'Born This Way'

Best Video With a Message 'Born This Way'

NME Awards

2010:   Best Dressed

Worst Dressed

2011:   Hero of the Year

Teen Choice Awards

2009:   Hook Up 'Just Dance' (feat. Colby O'Donis)

2010:   Female Artist

Summer Music Star – Female

Vh1 'Do Something!' Awards

2011:   Do Something Facebook

Virgin Media Music Awards

2009:   Shameless Publicity Seeker

Best Album *The Fame*

2010:   Best Collaboration (with Beyoncé)

World Music Awards

2010:   World's Best Pop/Rock Artist

World's Best New Artist

Best Selling Artist of America

World's Best Album of the Year *The Fame*

World's Best Song of the Year

Top Ten Memorable Outfits (to date)

1. Meat Dress (MTV Video Music Awards, 2010)
2. Kermit Dress (German talk show, July 2009)
3. Red Lace Dress (MTV VMAs, 2009)
4. *Phantom Of The Opera* Dress (VMAs, 2009)
5. Orbit Dress (Grammy Awards, 2010)
6. Lobster Hat (with chicken claw bracelet) (After-show party, February 2010)
7. Fire Bra Dress (MuchMusic Video Awards, 2009)
8. White Tiered Dress (BRIT Awards, 2010)
9. Bubble Dress (Fame Ball Tour, 2009)
10. Red Latex Elizabethan Dress (meeting Queen Elizabeth II, 2010)

Online

ladygaga.com:
Official site with info on Haus Of Gaga, news, events and lyrics

ladygaga.co.uk: Official UK site with a forum, gallery, shop and more

myspace.com/ladygaga: Check this site out for the Lady's latest songs, videos and tour updates

ladygaganow.net: Packed with resources for fans, such as interviews, videos, pictures and downloads

facebook.com/ladygaga: Check out Lady Gaga's latest writing on the wall

twitter.com/ladygaga: Join the 14 million other followers at @ladygaga

Biographies

Hugh Fielder (Author)

Hugh Fielder has been writing about rock and pop music for 35 years. He has witnessed and interviewed the great and the good, the not-so-good and the frankly useless. His appreciation of the power of pop goes back to when he took his daughters to see Madonna in her 80s heyday – twice. He is at a loss to explain why they later became such big fans of Wilson Phillips.

Malcolm Mackenzie (Foreword)

Malcolm Mackenzie is the editor of *We Love Pop*. He started as a professional pop fan writing for teen titles like *Top of the Pops*, *Bliss* and *TV Hits* before moving into the adult market working for *GQ*, *Glamour*, *Grazia*, *Attitude* and newspapers such as *The Times*, *The Sunday Times*, *The Guardian* and *thelondonpaper* where he was Music Editor for three years before returning to the teen sector to launch *We Love Pop*.

Picture Credits

All images © Getty Images: Marc Ausset-Lacroix/WireImage: 20; Neilson Barnard: 124; David Becker: 32; Michael Buckner: 102–3; Anita Bugge/WireImage: 97; ChinaFotoPress: 26; Giorgio Cosulich: 54–5; James Devaney/WireImage: 35, 53; Fairfax Media: 94–5; Logan Fazio/FilmMagic: 110–11; Charley Gallay: 70–1; Chris Gordon/WireImage: 86–7; Steve Granitz/WireImage: 112, 115; Scott Gries: 29; Handout: 57, 62–3; Dave Hogan: 123; Anwar Hussein: 65; Jakubaszek/WireImage: 73; Dimitrios Kambouris/WireImage: 78–9; Kevin Kane/WireImage: 66; Jeff Kravitz/FilmMagic: 108; David Livingston: 17, 80; Michael Loccisano: 89; Stephen Lovekin: 14–15; Larry Marano: 36, 85; Mike Marsland/WireImage: 69; Kevin Mazur/WireImage: 8, 12, 18, 41, 50, 82; Ethan Miller: 7; Paul Morigi/WireImage: 46–7; Oceanic Media Group: 30–1; Marc Piasecki/FilmMagic: 91; George Pimentel/WireImage: 11, 38–9, 48, 59; Chris Polk/WireImage: 100; Christopher Polk: 92; Bennett Raglin/WireImage: 44; Jun Sato/WireImage: 118–19; Andy Sheppard/Redferns: 116; Kristy Sparow/WireImage: 4; Jordan Strauss/WireImage: 107; Amy Sussman: 99; Aldrina Thirunagaran: 22–3; Brian To/FilmMagic: 105; Trago/FilmMagic: 74; Michael Tran/FilmMagic: 121; Jeff Vespa/WireImage: 24; Peter Wafzig: 61, 77; Andrew H. Walker/WireImage: 42.